CHARLOTTE BRONTË,
YOU RUINED MY LIFE

D1124798

ALSO BY BARBARA LOUISE UNGAR

Thrift
The Origin of the Milky Way

CHARLOTTE BRONTË, You Ruined My Life

POEMS BY

Barbara Louise Ungar

HILARY THAM CAPITAL COLLECTION
SELECTED BY DENISE DUHAMEL

THE WORD WORKS
WASHINGTON, D.C.

FIRST EDITION FIRST PRINTING
Charlotte Brontë, You Ruined My Life
Copyright © 2011 Barbara Louise Ungar

The Word Works
PO Box 42164
Washington, DC 20015

wordworksbooks.org
editor@wordworksbooks.org

Cover art: *Jane Eyre,* 1944
Used by permission, Twentieth Century Fox/Photofest
Book design: Susan Pearce

Library of Congress Catalog Number: 2010933680
International Standard Book Number: 978-0-915380-79-4

Acknowledgments

The following poems have appeared in the following periodicals
and anthologies:

Afterwards: Rosemary's Divorce

Chronogram: Looney Tune

Ekphrasis: The Brank

Every Drop of Water: Moccasins

The Nervous Breakdown: Rosemary's Divorce

Poemeleon: Like Being Alive Twice

Poems & Plays: Bad Demeter, Midsommer

Salmagundi: Unpacking, Charlotte Brontë, You Ruined My Life

Visiting Writers Anthology: Green Fire, Midsommer, Unpacking,
        Charlotte Brontë, You Ruined My Life

Grateful acknowledgment to the friends who read and helped with these
poems: Stuart Bartow, Naton Leslie, Frank Bidart and all the members
of his master class, especially Peg Boyers, Lee Gould and Ann Settle,
Paul Elisha, Sara Wiest, Ba Kaiser, Joe Kraussman, Miriam Herrera, Sue
Oringel, Marcie Newton, Djelloul and Marilyn Marbrook, Margo Mensing,
and Daniel Mandil. Special thanks to Denise Duhamel and Nancy White.
Thank you to The College of Saint Rose for sabbatical and release time to
complete this work.

For Sleeps in Hell

Vei Moci mai Heli

The poet must know how to hate.

—Goethe, quoted by George Eliot in Middlemarch

You wouldn't think one woman could marry two insane men
in one lifetime.

—Rita Hayworth to Glenn Ford in Gilda

CONTENTS

ROSEMARY'S DIVORCE

GHOST BRIDE

MYSTICAL THERAPY

ROSEMARY'S DIVORCE

Disengagement Ring

The wedding band, white gold,
didn't match. I began to pinch.
How did I get this misshapen?

Finally she pried me off, said
she'd get me fixed, then slipped
me on her little finger

as if trying to ditch me. Now
she's pawing through the trash,
the washer and dryer, beneath

the couch—I could be anywhere,
the grass, the bank, the gas station—
trying to retrace her steps

to yard sales, his pick-up
truck. She could turn the house
upside-down, accept the loss,

or live vigilant as a magpie,
always on the lookout
for my lustre …

After Chandidas

I throw ashes at all laws.

I did not burn his house down,
I just walked away.

What do I care
what my sisters say?

It was women
who crushed their daughters' bones

for a thousand years in China.
No law. Just the dictate of fashion.

I don't wear high heels.
I can run when I need to.

Unpacking

Leave the heaviest
        boxes till last:
                flat vermillion leaves

flutter from *The Italian*
        Painters of the Renaissance.
                Photos: twenty years old

at Dave's Luncheonette
        on Canal Street in your dress
                of handkerchiefs,

looking fresh off the boat
        from the old country
                of your childhood;

the shocking boy face
        of your first ex-husband;
                Grandma astride an ostrich.

A list of men from when
        you still numbered
                and remembered their names.

Dave's mosaic tile and famous
        eggcreams long gone
                but you remain

that greenhorn
        on the shore
                of your new address.

Charlotte Brontë, You Ruined My Life

A work is great, when it ceases to matter that it is bad.
—C. E. M. Joad

With his big cur and little French coquette,
his blind eye and depraved first wife, his locked
room, malignant mood and dungeon house—

Reader, I married him.

Big Sister of the Shelf, what shy bookworm
would not be staunch Jane and fall for
Mr. Mad-Bad-and-Dangerous-to-Know?

Beneath the mask, sardonic and harsh:
his brooding sorrow, his sordid
past, his rancid secret, which love alone

can lance. You infected me
as soon as I outgrew my horse books.
Charlotte, how many girls did you doom

to brutes? What could you know
of marriage? Yours killed you
in under a year. Childbed, thirty-nine.

Like Eyre, tenacious of life, I survived,
only I could not miraculously
cure him. Nearing fifty and divorce, I weep

as Orson Welles plays Rochester, those lines
I'd waited all my life to hear—

                                        As if
I had a string under my left rib,
inextricably knotted to yours . . .

and if we had to part, that cord
would be snapt; and I should take to
bleeding inwardly.

                        Goddamnit, Charlotte,
I married him.

Rosemary's Divorce

This is no dream—it's really happening!

What to do when you realize that handsome
devil you married wasn't just John Cassavetes
but an actual minion of Mephistopheles?
Not only have you been fucked by Satan,

but you've carried and nursed his spawn.
You are in love with Beelzebub's kid—
and, for the rest of your life, you *will*
have congress with the Prince of Darkness.

There is no escape. Your egg, his demon seed
intertwined in those golden curls,
the blue eyes you check daily for a goatish
sign, but find instead a Raphael,
a *bambino* fit for a Madonna.

Looney Tune

I've been gnawing this leg off
for years. *You made
your trap, now lie in it.*

You lie. He lies. She lies.
We lie. Half the double
beds in America will one day spring

shut with these steel teeth—
& kids get caught in the mangle.
Frantic, I worry my own

anklebone, while the hunter
draws his bead. Once
he chased me for sport, for my soft

pelt, his words like snares. Now
it's murder. Around
and around the court we go,

ridiculous Elmer Fudd
with his blunderbuss—*I'll get you,
you wascawy wabbit*—except

Bugs had no bunnies.

The Miller's Daughter

You appeared to help me spin
straw to gold. I promised, in

desperation. Little Man of Steel,
you call yourself: steel your hair,

steel your face, steely your
will to have your pound

of flesh. Hidden in your dark
house under the hill, you fondle

your hoard; at the forge you smelt
simulacra of my cunte.

A Mack truck, you'd love
to run me over. And over,

like a snake in your drive.
But I've become a clever Queane:

I've learnt your real name
so you can't steal my son—

Rumpelstiltskin—

go stamp your steel-toed boot
and tear yourself in two.

Mo' Bad Names for Women

It all began when Keva brought in her word
du jour: "harpy: a predatory monster
in classical mythology
having a woman's head
and the body and claws of a vulture;
an instrument of divine vengeance;
a shrewish or depraved woman."
Shrew begat virago, harridan,
bitch, cunt, ballbuster, and pigeon.

Synonyms for "whore" abound:
ho hooker harlot streetwalker slapper
prostitute concubine courtesan
slut tramp wench trull skank trick
cocktease siren trollop strumpet
Scarlet woman Jezebel vixen
nympho and her antonyms
frigid ice queen. Under "cow"

and "dog" came old-fashioned plain Jane,
wallflower, horseface, butch, scag,
busted, broke, slam-pig, fugly,
butterface (everything looks good but . . .)
Monet (looks good from far away but . . .)
and chickenhead (gives head a lot,
leading back to category two, ho.)

So we found women get put down
for three things mainly: sexuality (ho),
aggression (bitch) and looks (cow).
Later I realized we'd left out bimbo,
to which Keva added twat.

Gold Diggers of 2001

A sperm bank with a wallet,
you said that was how I saw you.

The precious ore once yours
I'd glimpsed only in old photographs—

that deep vein I wanted
alloyed with my own.

Not the coins you hoard
but the mine you squandered

drinking and blinding yourself.
Fool's gold.
> Your best friend says,

We used to look like Greek gods—
now we look like goddamn Greeks.

The gift I bore you
took for treachery—a trick, to loot

your life—when he sprang
all rose gold from my belly

while you slept
and Danaë wailed,

He stole my love!

Bad Names for Men, Too

Men are worms.
            —Bill Matthews

Let's start with the animals: dog, pig, snake,
weasel, skunk, rat, ape, mouse, wolf, ass,
old goat and hound dog. Then body parts:

schmuck, prick, dick, dickhead, peckerhead, dink;
asshole gives us shithead, shit, dipshit, scumbag,
douchebag, and jerk, jerkoff, dweeb, dumbass;
pussy leads to wuss, wimp, pussywhipped,
sissy, faggot, fag, fairy, cocksucker,
bitch, homo, queer, queen, fruitcake,
mama's boy, limp wrist, pantywaist
and girlyman. A small but popular
group gets at him through his mama:
bastard, son of a bitch, motherfucker.

When he ages, geezer, lecher, dirty old man.
Old-fashioned ones sound elegant:
blackguard, cad, rake, roué, heel, cuckold,
now almost obsolete, but still big
en Español, cabrón. Men, too,
get put down for three things mainly:
unkindness, stupidity, and femininity.

Not sex: call a guy a pimp, he might
take it as a compliment and say,
Don't hate the player, hate the game.

Statement of Net Worth

House:

     None

Car:

     None

Savings:

     None

Illusions:

     None

Debts:

     None

Insurance:

     None

Total Assets:

     Who can appraise
     the ruby inside?

     To him alone
     entrust it.

Why don't they just drop dead,

all these ex-husbands
of mine, instead of dogging me
like old tattoos, distorted

by wrinkles, faded & stretched by obscene
middle-age, humiliating me with my
unfortunate past lapses in taste.

Why do friends keep me posted:
the one who wouldn't give me a baby
has adopted two; the one who lied & cheated

for years publishes screeds on Virtue
online; the one who told me I ceased to exist
the moment he walked out of the room

charges 500 an hour for Tarot therapy in the Village.
I walked out of that room seventeen
years ago: why does *he* still exist?

The one who didn't want the kid
fights for custody, the millionaire
who repossessed my car pleads poverty.

Why does he have to call and poison
my exquisite hours? Why can't he keep his lousy
karma to himself? Why doesn't he drive

into a tree the way he threatened,
à la Jackson Pollock, only—please God—
with no innocent floozies in the car.

GHOST
BRIDE

What the Dream Makes Me Say

In my son's repeating nightmare
he's an alien with a blue face,
his sister's a ghost, his dada
a monster
    who sneaks up
invisibly
    & makes terrible sounds
he can't repeat or talk about—
that's the scary part.
     I know,
I try to comfort him. I know
too well what they sound like, but I can't
tell him how they drove me from that house.

Why can't you and Dada
marry again, he still sometimes asks.

I can't explain. (Can't tell him
I married a monster from outer space.)

Now he's afraid to fall asleep.

I tell him to punch the monster
in the face and say NO.
     I can't,
he says, *I can only say what the dream*
makes me say.
     I can only say
one word, like I-hate-you.

Crueler Than Disney

Binnie has to leave the house when *Bambi*'s on.
She takes her cigarettes outside.
Winter's here, the deer strip bark,
and we know what's coming.

Where's his Mommy, my boy asks,
more times than Bambi bleats *Mother*
through the blue woods, the blinding snow.
No answer avails. *I can't see her,*
he repeats, *Where is she,* as many times
as we have to watch this movie in a row.

They shouldn't let kids watch that, Binnie says
when she comes in, smelling of smoke.
Binnie has no kids, so she named her cat Ferne
after her mother who died of cancer.

My boy sung to sleep, I join Binnie
on the back porch. The cars pour, unseen, down
the highway, tributary to the river of death.
She smokes in the dark, I talk about Kristina,
who died when our boys were fifteen months old.
How we'd both found lumps: mine was
only milk. How the boy's father took him, like Bambi,
and we never saw him again.

Custodial Nightmares

1

You're perched in the crocodile's maw,
and though I scream, you remain
impossibly balanced, legs

outspread, playing Captain Hook—
& you're gone.

Mama!
I had the scariest dream. Someone
was trying to take you away from me.

Then I'm
picking you up from your father's
house, and I lie
beside you, love, and wake.

2

There was a witch
who liked to eat little children
and a cat made out of sand

and that cat made out of sand
could turn into anything.

The witch wanted to get you
but the sandman helped me save you.

3

A woman's arm twisted
like a corkscrew, cartoon-style,
her hand a burning wick.

4

I put my head inside an alligator's
jaws, to touch tongues: *Those who refuse*
to admit their shadow are condemned
to marry it.

5

Someone locked you in a room
and made you eat garbage
and I was the servant.

We got away, out the back
door, to our old house, but

I had to take you to the doctor
because you still like to eat garbage.

Against Disneyland

Disneyland is there to conceal the fact that it is the 'real' country, all of
'real' America, which is Disneyland.
                                        —Jean Beaudrillard

An iconography of excrement,
I might have said, at seven,
had I known the words.
Instead, I sulked in baleful silence

to torment my family all day.
Precocious, I knew how to ruin car trips
by getting carsick, but that was involuntary
genius; this, deliberate retribution:

How dare they bring me there?
I who scorned birthday parties,
even as a tot resisting
coerced laughter. Tiny pilgrim

dragged through the Inferno of California
sun on asphalt: each new line
descending to a deeper circle; each ride,
a worse contrapasso punishment.

A diminutive French critic,
lacking only a candy Gauloise Bleu
dangling from my disdainful lips:
My townspeople, what are you thinking!

No more Mickey Mousse,
I might have signified, had I
known how. Like any cartoon animal,
I recognized bad magic by instinct.

Instead, I simply cried.

The Middle-Aged Mermaid

Put out your little tongue, and I shall cut it off in payment; then your
tail will split in two, and every step you take will be like treading on a
sharp knife.

—Hans Christian Andersen, "The Little Mermaid"

I who undulated like an eel now mince on knife-point.

My iridescence vanished like a netted fish's—

blue water green water gold water black water silver
      clear water like light
below   all colors swam

Beached here
        dull as seaglass
                I'm ground

I do not recognize this hobbled creature
      her every step a swallowed tear
who limps down the marble stair at night
      to soothe her bleeding soles in brine

Other women gave up
              their tongues
                  their feet
their clits
      the breeze on their skin
                    & in their hair—

for love,
for love,
always for love.

Rembrandt's *Lucretia*

Look at her mouth,
crumpling like a child's about to cry.

Her half-shadowed face
haloed in lush hair and subtle gems.

Her gold robes spread like a bell
around her, white chemise

open from breastbone to belly,
echoing the slit, the cureless

wound she's carved on her
house fortress mansion temple tree.

The loving dagger still
clutched in her right hand,

she's painted the unseen
on her side in good red blood—

Vagina: Latin for scabbard.

Cerberus

Close your eyes, slowly step
   into the waiting
      boat and drift away

   where Ocean rolls
      a map of vastness

   inner constellations
      galaxies and spiral nebulae
         blue supernal light

The grizzled black dog,
   pacing, wraps his chain
      around your spine, barking
   I—*I*—*I*— all night

              Hush

the river of stillness flows within
   beneath stone streets

On its bank, the black dog worries his bone

The Brank

Lithograph, 1984, by Leon Golub, Am. b. 1922

In the museum of beautiful nudes,
why do I choose the most hideous?
I wanted those etchings
of women growing out of trees,
the lines of their bodies mirroring
hills, or boughs, or pears . . .

But this—shit brown, red
smeared like blood—this ugliness
won't shut up. Did they really
have those bunny ears, like some jokey
S & M costume, or Madonna's next tour?

Brank [etymology unknown. from Ir. *brancas,* halter?]
　　vb. (obs.) To prance; to hold up and toss the head;
　　　　applied to horses as spurning the bit. [Scot. & Prov. Eng.]

　　　gossip's bridle
　　　　dame's bridle
　　　　　hag's harness
　　　　　　witch's bridle
　　　　　　　scold's helm

　　　a Brydle for a curste queane

In a vast profusion of fantastical and sometimes artistic styles

A locking iron muzzle, metal mask, or cage,
  hinged to enclose the head
    often of great weight

The victim's mouth was clamped shut
  by an iron band under the chin
    a flat piece of iron forced

inside her mouth, sometimes sharpened
  to a point, or studded with spikes,
    spurs, or a rowel

        The whole contraption
fastened round the neck with a heavy padlock

The designs were left up to the imagination
  of the blacksmith

              Some shaped like pigs' heads
Some had asses' ears
        and huge spectacles
              Some,
a bell on a spring to draw jeers
          Some, a chain—

Ancient houses had a hook fixed beside the fireplace
  if she nagged too much the town
    gaoler would bring the community bridle

Every respectable settlement in England or Scotland had one

Sometimes she was drawn around town on a cart
  in the 'gagging chair' or 'tewe'

Sometimes the bit forced blood out
  at the slightest movement
    of the head or twitch of the halter

Sometimes she was led on a rope like a pack animal

Sometimes she was chained to the market-cross
  in the town square

Sometimes she was smeared with feces and urine

Sometimes wounded fatally,
  especially her breasts and between her legs

*And padlocked on women convicted of witchcraft
  so they could not scream their horrible curses
    while burning at the stake—*

All the nudes are speechless.

The Witching Hour

Quarter to four—
        time for crones' eyes
                to startle awake

hearts battering,
        sweat-drenched,
                all mother-sweetness drained away

The hour of spells, conjuring
        sleep, that small
                death

Deliver us from these
        bad dreams—seven
                dog paws severed in the bed

As succubae
        we soar
                over the snoring houses

enter their rooms
        on moonlight
                grab their penises—

just as they fear—
        carry them off
                and laugh

and laugh at the little men
        shrunken to worms
                in our liver-spotted hands

Ghost Brides

*The tradition, called 'minghun' or afterlife marriage, is common in
northern China, where a recently deceased woman is buried with a
bachelor to keep him company after his death. —AP*

Yang Dongyan, 35, a farmer,
bought a young woman for $1,600
to sell as a bride. Liu Shenghai
told him she was worth more dead.
Yang killed her in a ditch,
bagged her body, sold it
to Li Longsheng, undertaker,
for $2,077, minus a cut
for Liu. A 'less pretty' prostitute
brought only $1,000.

Every night the ghost brides come
to ravish the living bodies of Yang,
Liu, and Li, reenacting each detail
of murder, trade and burial, as foreplay,
murmuring, *You tried to sell me
to another, but I am yours forever.*

The brides lean in with ghastly lips,
devouring kisses, ride the men
relentlessly and laugh as hair and ribbons
of flesh peel off in foetid wind, come
in wave after wave of formaldehyde.
The men lie paralyzed beneath them
in that dream-stupor where you need
to run but can't move. They rise
gibbering from their beds, vowing never
again to sleep, but exhaustion
throws them back into that ditch
where the brides bide their time, panting
through their endless honeymoon.

In the Kitchen, Dead, for Two Years

Kathleen lay on the kitchen floor
for nearly two years her husband and son
stepping around the remains
as they prepared meals

Jack told police his mother
had fallen in the kitchen
sometime in mid-2003
and remained there

he left her in the kitchen
tried to feed her
and take care of her
for a couple weeks

the home was in disarray
littered with trash and cat
feces Kathleen's clothed remains
uncovered on the kitchen floor

Jack's father Harry eighty-one
returned home from a walk
as they were arresting his son and asked
Where's my wife?

Coming To

as if teletransported
                                from outer galaxies
all ninety-three trillion
                                cells come hurtling
                                                back into connection
dialing up
                consciousness
                                gathering
you don't know who
                        what
                                where you are
or *that* you are
                        human or speak English

struggling upstream
                        against—
                                        what

could this be
                        death?

—spiraling
                through primal
chaos to recon-
                struct and find your
                                        self (sick, happy
animal) condensed
                        in sweat on the cool
tile floor.

From a Magician's Midnight Sleeve

sprang these doves, dreams fluttering
like silk scarves drawn from the bottomless
hat of night. Bottomless, or false-
bottomed, a secret compartment
full of rotting eggs, extra aces,

disappeared ones nestled in black velvet
with the iridescent violet lining
of the skating skirt you bought for the twirled
beauty of its hidden hem, knowing
the waist was so tiny, it would never fit.

Genuine VOODOO GODDESS OF DIVORCE

Hand-crafted, Spellbound Voodoo Co., New Orleans

What gives, Voodoo doll?
Five years since I split the dollhouse
& I'm not divorced yet

You hide me in office

You were scaring my son—your skull
face, X-eyes, feather headdress—

You don't do me right

I lit a candle every night—

Desires say out loud

I can't, with my son there—

In your room,
in your bed?

Only after nightmares.

No hair, no photo, nothing of mister

I may not be a good Jew, but I'm Jew-
ish—

You stick pin in heart for good
but no stomach for bad

I don't want much—

No 'bad' for him?

He can't possess me—that will burn
till he dies.

We can speed that up

I don't want the guilt—

You tie my hands

47

You're just two bundles of straw
tied to crossed sticks
with calico & yarn.

Figure of speech, dodo

Can't you just get me divorced already?

Got powerful demons on his side

You mean his barracuda lawyer?

She work for me
Lawyer, judge, clerk   all work for me

You're helping him, too?

All call on me

But I WILL get divorced, someday?

By & by, honey, by & by

You got Luz divorced in six months—

Luz never let go
in that house for years
with his things   his dead wife's paintings

Were you the one who burned her house down?

Maybe yes
maybe no
Get hair or picture   incense
nine days   morning & night
stick pin in stomach   say desires loud

Till then
I never will speak word

MYSTICAL
THERAPY

Rescue

The dog of the soul whines to go out.

Out, out. Confined
within, she leaps up your chest,

bounding like a Jack Russell terrier.

Out. Panting for the leash. She lives
to run, to scent the keen air for invisible

traces. Bird dog. Flying dog. Her eagerness

can yank a strong man off his feet. Day after day
she waits, chin on paws, for you to come home.

She lives for the hour when you walk abroad.

Moccasins

Sky-blue beads' pattern of heaven
and walking on wind—
who made them?

When I left home
and the Great Plains behind,
I painted the floor of my narrow

room that very blue: I had
a futon, books and clothes,
three windows that opened on chains

into magnolia trees.
I lived in the sky.
I danced all night and out into the dawn.

It's those cloud moccasins
I want, dancing the sky

Operation Barbie

The children wanted to play doctor.
They chose an old Ballerina Barbie
whose leg was shot from years of soaring leaps
across the living room
and her phenomenal 360-degree rotation.
They stripped her, ripped her leg off
and shoved her between the couch cushions.
When she came to, she couldn't move.
They'd reattached her leg, but it didn't feel
plastic. She couldn't pee, so they tried
to catheterize her, but couldn't find a hole.
So they stuck her on a pink bed pan
in a gown of torn dish towel (that kept
slipping off), and ran outside to play.
When they thought of it, they ran back in
to prick and prod her. She couldn't sleep for weeks—
at the slightest sound, her stiff lashes
snapped. She tried to recite
Macbeth

> *Sleep that knits up the ravelled*
> *sleave of care*
>> was all that came.
She knew that "sleave" didn't mean sleeve and "ravelled"
didn't mean unraveled, but couldn't remember what they did mean.

She was so happy the day they bathed and dressed her
in one of her own bright flowered dresses
and a pair of supp-hose. And now
she chooses a fresh frock each day
and totters about the dollhouse
on flointed feet
learning to walk again.

She has a plan—
> *I'll run off*
& join the Béjart Ballet.

Kill Jar

On our long car trips I'd pluck butterflies
from the front grille at gas station stops &
keep their delicate corpses to ogle
& mourn in the back seat. Pure brilliance
to punctuate the monotony of telephone
wires scalloping the nauseous hours.

My father tried to teach me taxonomy,
to pin specimens to labeled mounts.
I listened, baffled. He bought me a net:
I liked running through summer grass
after their erratic paths; it was easy
not to catch anything. Then he handed me

a mason jar with a cotton ball
soaked in chloroform. I couldn't use it.
I dropped the kill jar on the back steps.
A cloying stink on the breeze.
My little sister fell, a shard
scarring her knee. And I quit trying.

Mystical Therapy

The Silver Fox sliced me open &
stapled me shut. After weeks in bed,
I am carried to a rare pine barren
where wild lupine bloom, last stand
of the Karner Blue. It is the last
day of May. I lean
on my stick. The hills
billow around me, a green
sea, a sunny tempest.
Wind roars through the trees,
trees rock, leaves shimmy, grasses
toss the blue air dizzy with golden
leaves, needles, spinners . . .

There is no still point. Seated
in the grasshoppers' din, I grip
my stick, tossed by the surge—
roiling, as in Van Gogh,
everything pouring
into everything else, sky into trees,
trees into sky, trying to tear
themselves up by the roots and sail away.

Drunk, almost seasick, with euphoria—
I can see
how, if this got louder or
brighter or more boisterous
or simply would not stop, like tinnitus,
it could be too much.

You could be blown away.

And where are the Karner Blues—
hidden deep,
clinging to small shelter.

Recovery

And the black wings lifted
off her shoulders

and the ravens withdrew
their beaks from her throat

and sailed off
trailing their rusted croaks

where the grey sea
broke over the sea wall

till beams of god-
lighting struck through the squall

She tried her new body
strange without pain

the long forced march ended
but she did not drop

as she thought she might—
the memory already winging

far and strange as those birds
now lost in forest night

Zen and the Art of Catch-and-Release

You practice all summer
in cold trout streams,
wading waist-deep
down the kill
while I work the rusted
hook from my jaw.

Sunbrowned, briarscratched,
you dream, rod in hand,
of a slight tug, the delirious
reeling in, then
the grappling slippery
slapping writhing free—

As cunningly as you tie
and cast your delicate
flies to lure the secret trout,
blood cooling in the icy creek,
tell me—

    Do you wait for me?

Spell

I want to lie down in your hand
I want to lie down in your eye
I want to lie down in your hair

want to lie down in your root
to lie down in your hold
down in your socket

in your green
in your sad
in your
book

Inferno, Canto V: Paolo & Francesca

We always knew we'd end up here, in the first
circle, destination of all lovers
caught in the carnal swift: how easy
to swim, blessèd fish, in the great
school of love, minnows and barracuda
flashing alongside, swept up in this current
which, from within, is clearly all there is.

Mermaid Love

We're fish from the waist down,
all sinuous tail and fluid thrashing.
You inhabit within yourself the tiny schools
swimming up their vast strait
and I am split like a flounder.

The human drains away
the further down we go,
submerged in the ancient
element whence we came
salt sharp wet. Like Thetis,

like Proteus, each changes shape
endlessly, matching the other,
centaur satyr siren, but mostly
human from the waist up
and submarine below.

Champagne and Pull-ups

I feel like Fred Astaire in *Royal Wedding*
gazing at a picture of his girl (not Ginger
Rogers) till he bounces lightly off the chair
& up the wall, across the ceiling, around
the chandelier, & down the other side,
crawls back up to break-dance on the ceiling
& down again, while my son laughs
out loud & says, *You know why*
he can dance on the ceiling? He has
gum on his shoes. And even though I knew
the crew had somehow turned the set a slow
360 degrees on its invisible axis
while he danced against gravity,
the effortless grace of the illusion
is the joy, whether the room be spinning
or still.

Tinker and His Rocket

Even at eight, I had you on my mind.
In my first novel, *Tinker's Adventures,*
I drew you as an elf, a gardening,
house-breaking trickster, with a mushroom cart

pulled by two white mice, Peeper and Peeker,
"piolet" of your own *"secret invention":*
Tinker's Rocket, anatomically
correct, in three stages, named Hopeful Pat,

to be launched from a pad *"between the barn*
and a clump of Lily of the Vally . . .
Tinker felt like he could burst of happie-
ness, but there were two important things,

getting training, and learning how to steer."
There, the fifteen-cent green spiral notebook
from Walgreen's filled, the manuscript breaks off—

The Stones Don't Care

Sleep, darling.
The white stones we stole from the river
bring a coolness, like shade
to the garden in full bloom.

Last night we almost had our first fight
but didn't. We stopped instead
at the oldest marble quarry in the country,
in Dorset, Vermont. A pair of lovers
sat on the hewn steps,
white blocks striated black
reflected in water dark and still,
ominously deep.

A gibbous moon.
A white cat with a few black marks
watched from a path as if cut from marble.

This morning a hummingbird
joined us at breakfast, sipping
red beebalm through her
needle mouth, treading air.

Stop thinking, *If only . . .* or
I'll be happy when . . .

Like Being Alive Twice

When you wrote the messages you heard in your sleep
  There is another life you might be living or
  Someone you never knew often wonders about you
they were my words

When you wrote
  He senses someone in search of him,
  his real body lost it was me

I flew eight thousand miles to Fiji
  wings between the thighs
but you had gone

You searched strange kitchens
  Doorways open in secret where ones
  we are yet to meet
  sleep naked under tables

Even after you gave up—
  where the one I am unable
  to stop loving
  gazes forever through me
I was on my way

While you traveled widely in Salem
  another earth
  where wanderers are happy
  in their lovesickness and sudden lunacy

Yes, I was walking barefoot by the purple Nile

Recipe for a Long, Happy Marriage

Ingredients: Find the right person.

Directions: Wait
till you can't stand it any longer.
Add love. Stir.
Cook in double
boiler over high flame
for several years:
stir constantly until
brought to a full rolling
boil. Add salt to taste,
water as needed. Just before
boiling over, lower
heat to simmer
gently. Stir occasionally. Add
spice to taste. Dust with cinnamon.
Garnish with pansies and nasturtium.

Serves two.

Schmucks

Grandma and Great Aunt Frieda said
at my first wedding,
We didn't think about being happy.

It was a job. You just hoped
he wasn't too mean or too cheap.
But he was. My first wasband

filled the house with a hundred roses
the first time he cheated, a string
of pearls after he confessed.

The second gave me a diamond
necklace, and a bouquet a day
for months—after I'd split. They both

took back the car. I've no idea
what happened to my first engagement
ring, although I know I lost

that diamond twice. (As I lost the pearl
in the ring from my paramour—
which he'd given to some other

woman first.) If that ring ever turns up,
I'll hock it, the way my second
wedding ring got melted down

as scrap. The second engagement
ring (with Grandma's diamonds)
wandered off on its own.

2

Diamonds go, like everything else,
only more slowly. Those had been hocked
to Grandma in the Great Depression.

Her generation knew how to hang on,
even when miserable, to the family jewels. Ach,
the world is lousy with schmucks. German

for jewelry, schmuck is also Yiddish
for dick, or a prick. Scarce as true
love, mensch is Yiddish for man, a real man.

Hope triumphing over experience
again, I'm having the latest regifted ring
resized and its lost pearl replaced.

Only Emily

Only Emily Brontë understands
why I chose to chain myself
to a demon.

           Heathcliff isn't a man,
Merle Oberon warned back in '39,
but something dark and horrible to live with.

You, Emily, planted the desire
for a demon lover in the frigid
tundra of my book-wormy youth.

Something reckless in me answered—
I wanted to be indomitable too.
We were both lonely, with no boys

but our wimpy brothers. Only prison
makes you free, you whispered,
and I enlisted.

           The mind-forged manacles
made manifest—in steel and Law,
Fatherhood and cash.

           No coward soul is mine,
you sang, and skipped off into immortality:
the girl who asked Daddy for a whip

and got Heathcliff—the fury
                    of scorned love,
an unmothered stone of rage.

You summoned him from hell and so
became him. I could never have dreamed
him up, so I married him instead.

Only those of us trapped in the flat
denouement of living have to go on
being degraded by your golem—

                              while you slip
free as Cathy ghosting the moors,
your hard mother's body, loved more
than life itself.

Barbie Turns 50

After passing for twenty all these years,
SURPRISE! Time
to get rid of the minis, skinny
jeans & skimpy tees, all those vintage
sundresses with teensy waists.
Even with my breast reduction,

suddenly I feel fuddy-duddy
as a dirndl next to the new Bratz,
those kiddie-porn tarts. I
always concealed my model,
a German doll, a professional
named Lulu—or was it Lili?

It's not just me—all my friends
    are desperate—
Midge, who looks fab, just had electro-
    shock for chronic depression,
Skipper's adorable but bulimic
    & deaf from decades in rock bands,
Ken's an alcoholic &
    GI Joe's on the street with PTSD.

You've got to face it when your parts
start to wear out. You're lucky if you can
still play, & luckier still if someone
wants to play with you. All the money
& drugs & plastic surgery in the *world*
can't save you. Just look
at what happened to poor Jacko.
We could all be recalled in a heartbeat.

Bad Demeter

Not that it doesn't hurt to watch her disappear
through that dark door, not that his shadow
doesn't chill me, too, but she goes willingly

and comes back unscathed—sometimes has nightmares
but who doesn't, and sometimes even
cries for him in summer heat . . .

These Sicilians imagine me cooped up
like some weepy housewife.
Not every place on Earth

hibernates while my girl plays below,
bringing a smile to those grim lips, as I
once—but, no—

            This winter, I'll cruise the South
Pacific, island-hopping with my paramour:
in our wake, hibiscus and sundrunk butterflies

so when my darling child returns, she finds me
full of spring, ready to burst north
shivering in my little March dress.

The Diamond Shoals Lightship

Windy Hatteras, pirate-haunted
   coast, weirdly unreachable—buried
      by sand, spars of ancient wrecks
revealed are swallowed up again.

     No lighthouse would last on The Diamond
        Shoals, an ever-changing sandbar off
           the Outer Banks, so a lightship followed
        the wandering bar to warn other boats.

          You have come so far, all this way, to know
            something of tide & wrack, something
              of navigation, of the treacherous
           shoals of shifting sand. Hundreds of ships

              have foundered here, millions
          of creatures labored a lifetime
              on the glittering vessels cast away
         here, to be ground back to sand, a lucky few

       plucked up to ornament some bookshelf.
          Strive on untiringly, the dying Buddha said.
            Don't follow me—Be your own light.
Even he was pummeled back into the sea,

the common lot, grave and mother.

Torch Song

To think I've been carrying a torch
for my self all these years
and didn't know it. I'd fallen

out of touch, sometime
around puberty, and although I
ran into my self now and then

across the decades, we always
seemed to be married to others.
Then, at the reunion, there we were.

I was still a teenager
to my self, while everyone else
looked beat and grey.

Suddenly I knew: *I* was the one
I should have married! How much
easier life would have been . . .

I could've spared my self years
of torment, but would I be my
self then—and what about the kids?

Still, we're giddy with the freshness
of finding each other again
at long last, and, although everything

in the world has conspired
to come between us, in the end,
nothing can. Even if I never

see my self again, I can lie
back in the open palm of love.

Midsommer

It's not either man you mourn—but the dream
of love, before you woke to find yourself
in bed with Bottom and his ass's head.

Would it be better never to awake
to this disgust at what you've taken in?

Or to run after one who flees from you
or away from one who wants you? Panting
in the sun, even now, you're drowsing off

again. The dream can never be rejoined—

yet, weary, you slip into a lucid
sleep: the beautiful, switched player you chase
through painted woods and streams turns suddenly

to face you, stop your crazy flight, and say,
wide awake, *My arms are always around you.*

Notes

In **After Chandidas,** the epigraph "I throw ashes at all laws" is the first line of a poem by Chandidas (c. 14th-15th Century CE), translated from Bengali by Deben Bhattacharya, in *Indian Love Poems*, edited by Meena Alexander. The poem ends, "I will set fire to this house/ And go away."

In **Charlotte Brontë, You Ruined My Life,** the italicized lines are from *Jane Eyre*.

In **Rosemary's Divorce,** the epigraph is from *Rosemary's Baby*, spoken by Mia Farrow, whose husband is played by John Cassavetes.

In **Against Disneyland,** the line *An iconography of excrement* is from Herbert Marcuse.

Rembrandt's *Lucretia* hangs in the Minneapolis Institute of Art.

In the **Kitchen, Dead, for Two Years** is a found poem, from a lost news clipping.

The title ***From a Magician's Midnight Sleeve*** is from Elizabeth Bishop's poem "Late Air."

In **Genuine Voodoo Goddess of Divorce,** the last line is Iago's.

Moccasins describes a pair displayed in the Minneapolis Institute of Art, c. 1880-1910, A'ani (Gros Ventre) or Nakoda (Assiniboine).

In **Tinker and His Rocket,** the spelling is intentionally childish.

The title ***Like Being Alive Twice*** is from Li Po's saying to Tu Fu, "Thank you for letting me read your new poems. It was like being alive twice." The italicized lines are from early work by Stuart Bartow.

In **Barbie Turns 50,** Jacko is Michael Jackson.

In the title **Midsommer,** the spelling is intentionally archaic.

Rescue is for Lola.

Recovery is for Binnie.

Recipe for a Long, Happy Marriage is for Jo and Tim.

ABOUT THE AUTHOR

Barbara Louise Ungar is the author of two previous collections of poetry, *Thrift* and *The Origin of the Milky Way*. The latter won the 2006 Gival Press Poetry Award, a Silver IPPY (Independent Publishers' Book Award), an Eric J. Hoffer Notable for Poetry Award, and the Adirondack Center for Writing Award for Best Book of Poetry 2007 (co-winner). She is an English professor at the College of Saint Rose in Albany, New York.

ABOUT THE HILARY THAM CAPITAL COLLECTION

The Hilary Tham Capital Collection (HTCC) is an imprint of The Word Works featuring juried selections from poets who volunteer to assist The Word Works in its mission to promote contemporary poetry. Judge Denise Duhamel selected the HTCC books for 2011.

Hilary Tham was the first author published in the Capital Collection imprint, in 1989. In 1994, when she became Word Works Editor-in-Chief, she revitalized the imprint. At the time of her death in 2005, Ms. Tham had paved the way for publication of thirteen additional Capital Collection titles. The series, renamed in her honor, continues to grow.

THE HILARY THAM CAPITAL COLLECTION

Mel Belin, *Flesh That Was Chrysalis*, 1999
Doris Brody, *Judging the Distance*, 2001
Sarah Browning, *Whiskey in the Garden of Eden*, 2007, 2nd printing 2011
Grace Cavalieri, *Pinecrest Rest Haven*, 1998
Christopher Conlon, *Gilbert and Garbo in Love*, 2003
    Mary Falls: Requiem for Mrs. Surratt, 2007
Donna Denizé, *Broken Like Job*, 2005
W. Perry Epes, *Nothing Happened*, 2010
James Hopkins, *Eight Pale Women*, 2003
Brandon Johnson, *Love's Skin*, 2006
Judith McCombs, *The Habit of Fire*, 2005
James McEwen, *Snake Country*, 1990
Miles David Moore, *The Bears of Paris*, 1995
    Rollercoaster, 2004
Kathi Morrison-Taylor, *By the Nest*, 2009
Michael Schaffner, *The Good Opinion of Squirrels*, 1996
Maria Terrone, *The Bodies We Were Loaned*, 2002
Hilary Tham, *Bad Names for Women*, 1989
    Counting, 2000
Barbara Ungar, *Charlotte Brontë, You Ruined My Life*, 2011
Jonathan Vaile, *Blue Cowboy*, 2005
Rosemary Winslow, *Green Bodies*, 2007
Michele Wolf, *Immersion*, 2011

ABOUT THE WORD WORKS

The Word Works, a nonprofit literary organization, publishes contemporary poetry in fine editions. Since 1981, it has sponsored the Washington Prize, a $1,500 award to an American or Canadian poet. Monthly since 1999, The Word Works has presented free literary programs in the Chevy Chase, MD, Café Muse series, and each summer, free poetry programs are held at the historic Joaquin Miller Cabin in Washington, DC's Rock Creek Park. Every year, two high school students debut in the Miller Cabin Series as winners of the Jacklyn Potter Young Poets Competition.

Since 1974, Word Works programs have included: "In the Shadow of the Capitol," a symposium and archival project on the African American intellectual community in segregated Washington, DC; the Gunston Arts Center Poetry Series (Ai, Carolyn Forché, and Stanley Kunitz, among others); the Poet Editor panel discussions at The Writer's Center (John Hollander, Maurice English, Anthony Hecht, Josephine Jacobsen, and others); and Master Class workshops (Agha Shahid Ali, Thomas Lux, Marilyn Nelson).

In 2011, The Word Works will have published 73 titles, including work from such authors as Deirdra Baldwin, Christopher Bursk, Barbara Goldberg, Edward Weismiller, and Mac Wellman. Currently, The Word Works publishes books and occasional anthologies under three imprints: the Washington Prize, the Hilary Tham Capital Collection, and International Editions.

As a 501(c)3 organization, The Word Works has received awards from the National Endowment for the Arts, National Endowment for the Humanities, DC Commission on the Arts & Humanities, Witter Bynner Foundation, The Writer's Center, Bell Atlantic, Batir Foundation, the David G. Taft Foundation, and others, including many generous private patrons. The Word Works has established an archive of artistic and administrative materials in the Washington Writers Archive housed in the George Washington University Gelman Library.

Please enclose a self-addressed, stamped envelope with all inquiries.

The Word Works
PO Box 42164
Washington, DC 20015

wordworksbooks.org
editor@wordworksbooks.org

OTHER AVAILABLE WORD WORKS BOOKS